LORD
OF THE
VALLEY

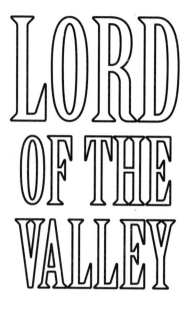

LORD OF THE VALLEY

HOPE FOR THE HURTING

JAMES R. SPRUCE

Beacon Hill Press of Kansas City
Kansas City, Missouri

10   9   8   7   6   5   4   3   2   1

Dedicated
with affection
to Karen
and our children
Darrin and Cynthia Grinder
Steven and Sharolyn

Contents

Foreword

Pastor Jim Spruce is my friend. We share a love of God, His world, His Word, and His children. We have worshiped together in comfortable, crowded sanctuaries and in the icy, wind-blasted solitude of mountain summits.

We were neighbors for a brief three years. We are "forever friends." Our love for God and mountains binds us together now just as certainly as climbing on Mount Rainier did in the past.

This book is filled with spiritual common sense. It is about godliness and real people. In these aspects it reflects the author.

Better than anyone I know, Pastor Spruce lives the balance between the spiritual and the material. He dwells completely "in the world" while avoiding being "of the world." His life is transparent with forgiven humanity and inward godliness equally visible at all times.

So, come meet my friend—Pastor Jim (never Dr. Spruce, although he has climbed that academic mountain). Hear him speak words of comfort and joy. Feel the love of God through him to you on these pages.

—Dr. George Harper, M.D.
Centralia, Wash.

Preface

Who can predict the course of misery? Wearing darkened lenses, misery is so blind that it bumps into all of us sooner or later. And it is so capricious as not to care.

But while heartache knows no limit, neither does God's grace. "Oh, the depth of the riches of the wisdom and knowledge of God! How unsearchable his judgments, and his paths beyond tracing out! 'Who has known the mind of the Lord?'" (Rom. 11:33-34).

Between grace on the one hand and misery on the other is the often frightful, and sometimes fatal, struggle for survival. It is like getting caught between a rock and a hard place. The hard place is misery. But guess who the "Rock" is?

When God, our Rock, is there for us, life is secure. But if "the heavens are brass" with God's silence, what then? Does He care? Does God help us triumph over what we face?

Pastors may give these devotional essays to those who suffer as shut-ins in homes, hospitals, or nursing care facilities. Yet all of us struggle with frailty. If we would let God find us, we would find Him and discover His presence: sometimes silent, sometimes specific, but always caring. Life can be cruel; yet, God rules and overrules! God creates wonder, both in His miracles and in His silence. Can we trust Him either way? Doubt has many a follower, but trust needs many a friend.

My thanks to Dr. George Harper, M.D., for lessons in climbing and in life; to Cynthia Grinder, my daughter and proofreader; and to my wife, Karen, who trusts His silence.

Pastor's Study
Flint Central

Acknowledgments

Christianity Today for a selection from "A Message from the Publisher," by Harold L. Myra, copyright 1985, by *Christianity Today.*

1 Acceptance

"You Are Accepted—Whoever You Are!"

WHO ARE YOU? Ah, there you are! Yes, I know you. I'd recognize you anywhere, for I am He who knit you in your mother's womb and who gave your life shape and substance. I knew all about you while you were yet a dream to others.

WHO ARE YOU? Why, you are no stranger to Me. I've watched you, cared for you, ached for you, pulled for you, planned for you, done for you . . . died for you. Without a doubt, you are My precious child!

WHO ARE YOU? You may have nearly forgotten who you are yourself, languishing so long there upon your bed of miseries. But I'd recognize you anywhere—even here. Here with your wires and tubes extending, here with your medications, here with your hurts and woes. Some may not recognize you. But I do!

WHO ARE YOU? Propped up there in bed like that, unable to do the things you used to do, unable to remember . . . and sometimes wishing you could forget. You who suffer, you who wonder and wait. You who'd like to be home again, and you who've no place but this to call home. Never forget: I see you where you are.

WHO ARE YOU? Locked up in your little place. Again, you say? Wanting to be free, wanting to get out, wanting to be left alone. Did you think I have not heard your anguish?

WHO ARE YOU? You with your aching joints, your

numbing pain, your tired body, your fearful heart. You who live with restless nights and tasteless food, with unwanted procedures. The loss of privacy and control.

YES, I KNOW WHO YOU ARE! And I accept you just the way you are. In fact, it is because you are who YOU are that I am who I am. Without Me, there would not be you. And without you, what need would there be for Me? See how much you mean—to Me? Yes, I know who you are. But . . . do you know who I am?

SOMETIMES THEY CALL ME GOD. That is who I am: Creator, Maker, Eternal One, Sovereign, King. I am given many names, for I have many things to do. My names represent My limitless capacity to know all things, be everywhere at once, and have all power necessary. That is why I am God. But I am more—for you.

SOMETIMES THEY CALL ME JESUS. Wonderful Counselor, Mighty God, Everlasting Father, Prince of Peace, Savior, Lord, Judge. In My Son I have offered ultimate acceptance, love, and forgiveness. It doesn't matter to Me who or where you are, what you've done or failed to do—I could not love you more than I do now. Sick or well, young or old, good or bad. You are accepted just as you are. Judged by your faith and works—yes, yes. But loved? Yes. My love is freely given. You need not work to "earn" it. That is why I am Jesus. But I am more—for you.

SOMETIMES THEY CALL ME COMFORTER. Spirit, Counselor, Advocate, Convictor, Convincer, Persuader. You are accepted as you are. You are forgiven for what you were. You are loved for what you will become. My acceptance of you includes making you more like Me. But I comfort you with an everlasting and reforming love for your good to make you an example (in your misery) of My grace! That is why I am Comforter. But I am more—for you.

SOMETIMES THEY CALL ME FATHER. That is what I want most to be to you. Look at your world and call Me Creator. Face Me in eternity and you will call Me Judge. But to call Me Father—that is your choice. It would be My highest honor for you to call Me Father. I can wait. Wait. That is why I am called the "Waiting Father."

DO YOU SEE ME NOW? Watching and waiting for you. Longing and hoping for you. Pulling and giving for you. I know all about you, I see your discomfort and distress, I bear your pain and misfortune, I am your Father in heaven.

BUT PLEASE UNDERSTAND: I long to be your Father-in-residence, offering the only thing nobody else ever fully offered: acceptance. You are accepted, whoever you are. "You are precious and honored in my sight" (Isa. 43:4).

Sometimes they call Me Father. Would you?

2 Aging

Bearing Up with New Wrinkles in Old Skin

Have you ever thought about what you'd like to have on your tombstone? Here's Benjamin Franklin's epitaph:

The body of Benjamin Franklin, Printer, Like the Covering of an old Book, Its contents torn out and stript of its Lettering and Guilding, Lies here, Food for Worms.

But the work shall not be lost; It will, as he believed, appear once more, In a new and more beautiful Edition,—Corrected and amended By the Author.[1]

Aging? Well, yes. But more. We are in a constant state of change. From the cradle to the grave there is an absolute guarantee: There will always be new wrinkles in our old skin. We are going through revision and are usually unaware of it until we get on the scales, look in the mirror, or attend a reunion.

Aging would not be so bad if you didn't have to get old to do it. But getting old means things either don't fit or don't work right. It means you can't go where you want, remember what you did, and sometimes don't feel good enough to care. It means the ones you used to care for are now supposed to care for you. It means you don't have the final say anymore. Not fair.

But for all the hardships aging brings, it is the slow justice of God. He is doing what He wills to do: correct and amend us for our appearance in our "final edition"—a glorified body. When you look at it like that, then aging becomes an honor—as if God was doing something necessary for the day when we make our grand appearance at His banquet in heaven's great festival.

Now, here on earth, we are going through all this misery: old age, sickness, loss of family and friends, heartache. But if we see it as part of the revision and remodeling that the Holy Spirit permits and even designs, then it has purpose.

Here is the big question: Will you give God complete access to your attitude and personhood as He does the remodeling? We know that the bodily changes will occur whether we like it or not. But something good happens when we consciously "permit" God to shape us according to His will. That is, when we tell God it is OK for Him to shape and reshape our mind, heart, soul, body, and being, we then become flexible and pliable in His gentle hands. The aging process makes anything brittle and stiff. But when we say to the Lord that we are "willing to be made willing" for Him to correct and amend us, our spirit becomes teachable.

I read once of a sculptor who intended to create a lion out of a block of marble. He had just begun chiseling when someone asked him how he thought he could make a lion out of a huge rock. The sculptor said, "I intend to chisel away everything that does not resemble a lion."

What if we gave God that kind of access to our spiritual life? What if we told the Lord that He could chip away anything in us that did not resemble His Son, Jesus?

Aging is not always pleasant. Many revisions are introduced, and many corrections are made along the way. How true in all of life! But if we give God the freedom to amend and modify as He chooses, how much more of a blessing we will be to Him and those around us. Painful? Certainly. It is not fun to be chipped on, to remain accountable to others, to keep the attitude we should while living with physical pain and change.

But remember! The author and perfecter of our faith (Heb. 12:2) is sculpting in us the very work that is on constant display in this life until its final unveiling on the day of His appearing. The Bible says, "And we . . . are being transformed into his likeness with ever-increasing glory, which comes from the Lord, who is the Spirit" (2 Cor. 3:18).

Are you aging? It just means you're looking more and more like your Father every day. You think you're getting old? God is called "the Ancient of Days" (Dan. 7:9)!

3 Anger

When It Isn't Fair and Can't Be Fixed

He waited in line at the airport ticket counter to confirm his reservation. Finally, as he spoke with the customer service agent, a bomb exploded. Someone had planted it inside the counter. When the timing device finished its cycle, the bomb went off.

Some were killed. He was wounded. In fact, he lost a leg. And all he wanted to do was check his luggage.

During a lengthy convalescence, he balanced upon the raw edge of confusion and anger. As a minister, he knew anger had to be resolved, but as a human being, he knew anger was real! He could not hide and deny his anger. Neither could he save it for future demolition work.

Then one day it dawned on him: He could not change his condition. Nothing he could ever do would restore his leg. That was the day he knew he had a choice: He could be destroyed by his bitterness or he could do something about it. He believed he had four choices regarding this new hurt: curse it, nurse it, rehearse it, or reverse it. Three of the choices were easy to fulfill, and one would bring him plenty of satisfaction.

If he cursed his problem and those who caused it, he would find ample opportunity to spill his vengeance. If he nursed his plight long enough, he would get lots of pity, both deserved and finally undeserved. If he rehearsed his situation, he could very easily make himself even more sick and have even more attention.

But one option would make rugged demands of him. If he chose to reverse negative and destructive attitudes into positive and constructive attitudes, not only would he become productive again, but life would be better for those around him as well.

Isn't it true of all of us? Life goes along quite well. Then suddenly some bomb goes off somewhere. We are laid low with an illness. Financial reserves dwindle. Someone we love dies. And we feel like shouting to the whole world: "Hey, this isn't fair!" And as if that were not enough, we also know that there is absolutely no way to restore things that once were.

Life is *not* fair. Unjust and unnecessary tragedies happen every day. Absolutely no human sense can be made from the random or intentional hurts that come our way. And we feel helpless when we know that we cannot fix or repair what has happened.

But it will help us if we remember that, while life is not fair, God still is. Part of our healing involves remembering that God's loving care does not guarantee His direct control. God is not required to do something for us just because we know we need it—or because He is God. His loving mercy for us is not based only on our need but upon His ultimate purpose.

God finds no pleasure in the things that break our

world. He neither causes nor dispenses them. He permits them. His perfect will is not the same thing as His permissive will.

How could a fair God allow things that are not fair? We have struggled with that question since the Garden of Eden. God does not need to reveal His justice in our lifetime. He is still God regardless of when or how or to whom He displays His mighty power. God created good, not evil, and He often lets the consequence of man's evil run its course. Bad things are here with us because of sin, which changed the rules of our relationship with God. Thus, His justice is not displayed in every airport . . . or in every hospital. When it isn't fair, you can tell God. He'll understand and agree. You can tell the Lord anything. It is because God already knows that He is able to care so much.

This is not so much for God's information as it is for our good. Otherwise, all the hurts, injustices, and other "bombs" that have gone off around you can turn you into an angry, bitter individual—mad at your loss and mad at your Lord.

Reversing the attitude of anger means letting go of the situation that irritates you by releasing it to God. Paul wrote, "Get rid of all bitterness, rage and anger" (Eph. 4:31). As you let go, you will be freed of anger. If you do not release your hurt and anger, it may eventually cost you more than an arm or a leg.

4 **Cheer**

On the Way to Preach, I Tripped

If you are crazy enough to laugh at the wacky things that happen to you, perhaps you won't go insane. If you're not, perhaps you already are.

In one pastorate, on a Sunday morning no less and

on an errand before preaching, I fell down a flight of stairs in the church. I heard someone say, "What was that?" but nobody came. I went to the hospital, got five stitches in a finger, and made it back to preach. The sermon was titled (prophetically?) "Marching Off the Map."

In yet another place of service I visited a man in the hospital who reached into his robe and pulled out a bottle filled with gallstones. He offered me one. "Only one?" I asked.

Once during church a parishioner reminisced about an old problem. Next he began to reveal the role of another person involved in the dispute. Before I could say anything, he said, "And just so everybody knows who I'm talking about, it was . . ." At that very moment his upper teeth flew out of his mouth, midsentence, bounced on the empty wooden pew in front of him, and fell rolling onto the tile floor. I stood there looking at a very silent witness with his smile in the aisle. He bent over to hunt up his teeth and his glasses fell off. At that point he hardly knew where to look for either. He was healthy enough to laugh with us, pick up his attachments, and apologize.

While teaching a class of young adults before the preaching service, I reached for my billfold. Suddenly my zipper broke from stem to stern. (Worst case scenario, friend.) Unfortunately, I was standing and there was no lectern. (Sometimes you can run, but you can't hide.) Nobody ever said a word except the man who told me his wife had gone home to get another pair of trousers.

At Centralia (may the Lord forgive them), a wonderful Thanksgiving dinner was given by the church board in appreciation for the pastoral staff. After the meal it turned into a royal roast of the "honored turkeys"—the pastoral staff. No mercy was shown. To celebrate my 50th birthday, the good folks here at Flint Central escorted me across town to the restaurant—in a hearse! It was wild, but I got to ride in the front seat. It helps if you can laugh at yourself because at least you can join the crowd.

You never know what will happen, even on your journey to serve the Lord. At this very moment nothing in your life may seem worth laughing about, and perhaps the best thing to do at times is to cry. But don't let the devil rob you of all joy. Always remember this short but powerful little verse: "A cheerful heart is good medicine, but a crushed spirit dries up the bones" (Prov. 17:22).

You may have a lot of drugs, medications, and all kinds of therapies to endure. But remember this magnificent prescription from the Word of God: Having a heart (or attitude) that can be cheered is good medicine for you. This does not mean that you always have to have a "stiff upper lip" or that you must "grin and bear it." No—break down when you need to. Get your feelings out with someone who cares.

But it does mean that whatever cheers us is good for us. Is it not all right to release ourselves to the ridiculous? Tough things, bad news, heartbreaks will all come our way. But if they come they will also diminish and finally vanish in time.

Zippers and flying teeth, stitches and gallstones: If you laugh at everything, people will think something is wrong with you. If you laugh at nothing, something is wrong with you. The difference between comedy and tragedy is the distance you are from it. If it is your zipper that broke, it's a kick. If it is mine that broke, well . . . That's all the more reason why the man with flying teeth who laughed along with the rest of us was such a good sport. He was able to be cheered in chagrin.

Open your eyes and ears. Has God allowed something that knocked you off your feet? While you're still in that position, perhaps He'll show you something that will crack you up.

Half a set of teeth in the aisle did it for me.

5 Contentment
"It Is Enough If You Don't Freeze"

Aleksandr Solzhenitsyn, recipient of the Nobel peace prize for literature, reflected upon his years as a prisoner in his native Russia:

> Don't be afraid of misfortune and do not yearn after happiness. It is, after all, the same. The bitter doesn't last forever, and the sweet never fills the cup to overflowing. It is enough if you don't freeze in the cold and if hunger and thirst don't claw at your sides. If your back isn't broken, if your feet can walk, if both arms work, if both eyes can see, and if both ears can hear, then whom should you envy? And why? Our envy of others devours us most of all. Rub your eyes and purify your heart and prize above all else in the world those who love you and wish you well.[2]

If it were not for name, nationality, and century, that could nearly pass as a loose paraphrase of something Paul might write. In fact, hear Paul's words from Phil. 4:11-13: "I have learned to be content whatever the circumstances. I know what it is to be in need, and I know what it is to have plenty. I have learned the secret of being content in any and every situation, whether well fed or hungry, whether living in plenty or in want. I can do everything through him who gives me strength." But look at these life applications from the Bible:

1. *Contentment is a learned discipline.* We don't inherit it from our parents, nor is it bestowed upon us from God as a spiritual gift. God helps us find contentment and rest

in both His will and our circumstance. But we offer the availability, the resolve, and the self-discipline it takes to face life's "whatever!" Neither Paul nor Solzhenitsyn nor any other faithful pilgrim on his or her journey with the Lord could learn contentment without experiencing tough times. We hate to say it, but comfort is less of a teacher than discomfort. Nobody wants hard times, but few of us learn the disciplines of contentment in easy times.

2. *Contentment is independent of circumstances.* Great saints like Paul discovered that contentment derives from the decision to see misfortune and fortune as about equal: neither lasts forever and neither completely makes or breaks life. Contentment, along with being a state of mind, does not rest on creature-comfort as the wellspring of hope. Physical surroundings, blessings and benefits, bells and whistles—none of them made much difference to Paul. Life goes on anyway, right? And that's the point: If contentment can be had without them, most of the things we need or want are nice but not essential to true happiness.

3. *Christ is the source of our strength in being content.* Here's the secret to Paul's great comfort in the middle of his great discomfort. Disowned, alienated, beaten, ship-wrecked, and imprisoned, Paul went through it all. But he survived long enough to write a truly memorable verse. "I can do everything through him who gives me strength" (v. 13). None of us can ever claim that contentment is something we do alone. We provide the availability; God provides capability. Without God, all we have is the failing arm of flesh.

One of the great heroines of my youth was Isabel Carnes. All the kids at Canton (Ohio) First call her Izzie. We knew she loved us because she never grew impatient. We put rocks in her hubcaps, and threw toilet paper over her trees. But every Saturday night, there she was: fixing chili, making pizza, offering her car to drive us around. I never knew it then, but Izzie had a pretty tough life all those years. Really tough. But she so rested her case with

God that her ability to serve others was not weighted with the baggage of discontent.

Like the Philippians, like Solzhenitsyn, like Paul, like Izzie, contentment can be found when in the stormy Dire Straits.

6 Courage

Nearly Every Alley Has a "Bully"

When growing up in Texarkana, mother used to send Sallye and me on errands to Palmer's Grocery. My younger sister was the responsible one and carried the money. I was the brave older brother and went along to make sure we bought a carton of mixed beverages: Royal Crown, Nehi Strawberry, Grapette.

We always took the shortcut down the alley, and, of course, had to remember Bully. Bully was Roger's mean-tempered dog, which accounted for my presence. He was always on a leash, which accounted for my bravery. I remember his shrill barking to this day. It was difficult to walk quietly on gravel, so we usually awakened Bully. We heard him coming, feet clawing and chain rattling, before he barked. Suddenly, he'd reach the end of his chain and flip 180 degrees in the air, landing on all fours.

Perhaps Bully marveled at my stupidity, coming so close to such danger. But then, I used to wonder if he ever tired of a stiff neck. Once Roger's mother called to tell us Bully had escaped. I stayed indoors for two days. So much for courage.

A lot of alleys and roads that people travel take a small amount of courage, especially when trouble is chained up and can only go so far. But when trouble is unleashed on your path and there seems to be no escape, then courage becomes essential for survival.

Dr. L. T. Corlett was in his last year as president of

Nazarene Theological Seminary during my first year. He frequently repeated a theme in chapel that stuck with us: "Gentlemen, whatever else you do, remember to thank God and take courage!" He often recounted Paul's shipwreck off the shore of Malta: "So keep up your courage, men, for I have faith in God" (Acts 27:25).

Well, it all sounded noble, and certainly brave, to me. I was young, idealistic, and pretty much unscathed at the time. Then came "life" after graduation. Now, looking back on nearly a quarter century of pastoral ministry, and having seen firsthand the devastation that trouble creates in the lives of people, I appreciate more clearly Dr. Corlett's admonition in light of the next verse. Paul wrote, "Nevertheless, we must run aground on some island" (v. 26).

Running aground and swimming for shore doesn't make a lot of sense unless it is our last option. We look for other alternatives, some other way wherein we have more control over how close we come to trouble (danger, heartache, sorrow). How difficult it is to believe that courage is commanded.

At this moment, you may feel the full force of some great trial or tribulation. Perhaps you are chased by some bully or are in the midst of swimming for your physical, emotional, or spiritual life. If so, remember the simple words of Jesus as He walked on the water toward the disciples' boat: "Take courage! It is I. Don't be afraid" (Mark 6:50).

First, remember that you are not alone. As God told Joshua, "Have I not commanded you? Be strong and courageous. Do not be terrified; do not be discouraged, for the Lord your God will be with you wherever you go" (Josh. 1:9). God never abandons us to suffer alone! He is always there with us.

Second, remember that you may not control the kind or amount of trouble that haunts you, but you can control your response to it. Not only is courage a biblical command, but it is also a necessary choice. You can choose courage as opposed to fear. You may not be spared from all suffering, but you do have some choice as to your attitude and response toward what comes.

If we go through life exercising reasonable caution, it will help. But we cannot avoid all bullies or all shipwrecks. Sooner or later, we shall meet up with one or another. The Christian's hope is not isolation from inevitable trouble (much as we wish it were) but appreciation for the inevitable presence of Jesus Christ.

So, thank God and take courage!

7 Death

The Marbled Angel of Scottsville

We knew it was there, just across the fence and not 50 yards from the old wood-shingled tabernacle at Scottsville. Somewhere in the ancient cemetery, shrouded in mystery and weeds, was what we called "the angel." Only a few older kids privately bragged that they had seen it. The cemetery was off-limits to children.

Every year our family traveled from Texarkana to Scottsville to attend camp meeting. Just east of Marshall, Tex., Scottsville was a landmark holiness camp founded before the turn of the century. My grandfather, father, and I knelt at its altars across the generations.

We talked a lot about "the angel," a marble statue over one of the graves. One year, curiosity got the better of me. I climbed the fence and entered forbidden territory. At last I came upon the site.

There stood the angel above a simple grave: tall and elegant, white and ghostly. Its wings were opened slightly, its chiseled face seemed to be in prayer. The angel's hands rested just above the head of a small child. And on the marker these words: "If love couldst have saved thee, thou wouldst not have died."

The story was that the child of very wealthy parents lingered in illness for some time before dying. Naturally, their love would have paid any price. But understandably, love cannot purchase length of life.

Death. It is the first enemy when life begins. It is the last friend when life ends. It is the only bridge between the opposite worlds of time and eternity. It finds little comfort in the vocabulary of those who wish to live.

The trouble with death is dying. When you're dead it's all over, and the misery you had in this world is finished. But before you're dead you're dying, and dying we don't like. If you could die quickly in your sleep, that would help. But since we cannot, and must not, control the time and way we die, then we have to face dying. God must be allowed to be God in death.

Strange, isn't it? We all know we are going to die someday. But knowing an approximate time frame, say six months to two years, makes us begin the dying countdown process. In reality, God began the countdown for us at the moment of our conception. We should honor God's timetable for our last breath. He knows when and He knows how.

Death. It has not only a finality but also a timing. It is the last moment in this life and the first in the life to come.

Would you like to have an inspired affirmation from the Psalms regarding timing? Hear it: "My times are in your hands" (Ps. 31:15). What a wonderfully encouraging thought! God knows our beginning from our ending. He has them separated at just the right distance. How simple. How profound.

Somewhere between the perfect and the permissible will of God, our time shall come. Can we trust Him with that? To have the confidence and courage to place your own times in the hands of God frees you from fretting about "when."

One of the most important questions I've had to re-solve in my life is this: Do I believe God knows what He is doing? It is not sacrilegious. It is a struggle of my frail humanity. I have come to believe that God knows exactly what He's up to. In most things He's chosen not to inform me. But I know He knows.

If He knew when to let my life begin, why shouldn't He know when to let it end? If I trusted Him with my life, why shouldn't I trust Him with my death? If I trust Him with me, can I trust Him with those I love so dearly?

Marbled angels? Sure. What love wouldn't do to spare hurt! If you have ever thought God's gift of physical life was so great, look what He did for an encore.

8 Defeat

The One Thing Worse than Failure

C. W. Longnecker wrote these words:
> If you think you are beaten, you are;
>> If you think you dare not, you don't.
> If you'd like to win, but think you can't,
>> It's almost a cinch that you won't.
> If you think you'll lose, you're lost,
>> For out in the world we find
> Success begins with a fellow's will—
>> It's all in the state of the mind.
> Life's battles don't always go
>> To the stronger or faster man;
> But sooner or later the man who wins
>> Is the man who thinks he can![3]

There really is one thing worse than failure. It is defeat. Failure is an attempt that went wrong. Defeat is an attitude of resignation before an attempt is made. Because you have to try, it takes a certain amount of courage to fail. Defeat, however, takes neither courage nor effort. It means giving up before you start.

A friend was convinced that his job could not accomplish a particular challenge. Nothing could be said to change his mind. In fact, he wanted no part of it. Regardless of how much momentum other people created, he said it would never work. When the day came and victory was achieved, he said it wouldn't be long before the dream would tarnish and die.

How tragic. A defeatist attitude does wonders to destroy hope and demoralize confidence. It is interesting that circumstances are not the barrier. Sometimes there are many hindrances to victory, and failure does occur. But the big enemy is attitude—or what and how we think.

This is not an appeal for our effort only at the neglect of what God can do. Nothing is done by us without God's direct or permissive will. But it is an appeal to remember that we should cooperate with God by having a confident mind-set toward His will and way. The Bible is not in conflict with a positive mental attitude. We really are what we think. Paul encouraged the Philippian church: "Finally, brothers, whatever is true, whatever is noble, whatever is right, whatever is pure, whatever is lovely, whatever is admirable—if anything is excellent or praiseworthy—think about such things" (Phil. 4:8).

Do you face some hard trial? Has some unexpected turn surprised you? Have burdens weighted you down? Without a doubt, life can be counted on to bring us all the trouble we need. Failure, in any of its many forms, seems to be our lot sooner or later. But failure is not defeat. Athletic teams may be defeated in competition but indomitable in spirit. At least the losing team was on the field and tried.

God knows we may fail. He knows we may get defeated. See how it happens from those two sentences? Failure is an occurrence while defeat is a process. Failure is an event in time while defeat becomes a way of life.

The idea is not a success theology in which we claim a privileged right to promised victory. Who wins or loses is very important in our culture, but it is far from the complete picture. If somebody has to win, then somebody has to lose. We dare not measure our value to God, others, or ourselves in such ways. Attitude determines how we handle life's failures.

But our confidence is in God, not self. Paul said, "I can do everything through him who gives me strength" (Phil. 4:13). It is God who gives the strength. But we must be the willing "I can" vessel through which He flows.

It can be tough to develop an attitude of such confidence—confidence that is born of God, tempered by trial, and proven by determination. But you and God are a majority.

9 Depression

Have You Been Through the Wringer?

There it stood: gurgling and swishing, churning and moaning right in the middle of our basement. Upright on four sturdy legs, with its cord plugged into the wall socket. Mother absolutely forbade me to go near it!

I was fascinated, frightened, and nearly hypnotized by the magnetic spell this creature cast over me. It was a new washing machine with a special feature, purchased by Quindaro Church of the Nazarene for their parsonage.

Like a steel sentinel, it cast an imposing pall upon my childish curiosity for one reason: The special feature was an automatic wringer.

The wringer looked like two large rolling pins. Unlike the old hand-cranked wringers, these rolled automatically. Clothes could be put through, wrung dry, and come out flat as a pancake. What fun it was to watch mother put sheets through and see them come out stiff as a board!

But she always warned me, "Whatever you do, never

put your fingers in that wringer while it's going. You might wind up with your arm wrung out!" Well, I was a pretty hard case at times, but flat underwear was enough to convince me. The phrase "been through the wringer" has always carried a certain amount of credibility with me.

Funny memory. Not so funny expression. Millions of people, at one time or another, have felt like they have been through the wringer. Feelings of hopelessness, sadness, loss, shame, anger, and exhaustion are used to describe our frame of mind when we have been through it. Yet another word we often use when in the grip of negative emotions that seem beyond our control is depression. For most of us, fortunately, depression does not last too long and is just a "case of the blues." But for a certain percent, depression may be life-threatening. There are no quick cures, but there are some helpful things to remember.

First, depression is real. Some mistakenly think depression is unspiritual and Christians ought to simply "snap out of it." A victim of polio would not be so advised. So try to be understanding with people who think emotional pain is insignificant. Try also to be fair with yourself. You are a complex whole: spiritual, physical, emotional, mental. We admit physical needs; likewise, we need to admit spiritual, emotional, and mental needs.

Second, God would understand if you went to Him with serious depression. You wouldn't be the first. David's great sin, Elijah's wish to die, and Job's turmoil were opportunities for God to deal with suffering and depression. Sometimes God heals us quickly, sometimes slowly. His will must be our first consideration. Then we must trust Him however and whenever He brings help.

Third, God often uses skilled professionals to aid our healing. Psychiatrists, physicians, psychologists, counselors, pastors, and other trained professionals are available. Many find that medication, when properly supervised, eliminates their depression. The wise advice of godly and mature friends may help.

Fourth, never underestimate your own part even when depressed. At your darkest hour, when you turn to God in prayer, He will be there. But don't wait until things are at their worst to turn to God. If you can turn to Him anytime, turn to Him many times. The Psalmist wrote, "Why are you downcast, O my soul? . . . Put your hope in God" (Ps. 42:5). Stay in touch with your emotions. Let God know how you feel. Faith in God does wonders for your mental attitude, which must remain positive.

Last, by all means, if you feel suicidal tell God and another trusted human being. Life's wringers squeeze pretty hard. The shifting morals of our culture may make suicide or euthanasia quite attractive, and you will need to remember that, even if nobody else cares for you, God does. He has paid a great price for your ability to hold on, especially after you've been through a few wringers. Be cheered. God rules . . . and overrules.

10 Disappointment

Rainier: Where Hope and Hardship Meet

The narrow road turned sharply to the right, and there was Mount Rainier, broad-shouldered and bathed in the glow of a midnight moon. Our conversation hushed in respect for the sentinel's Maker. The mountain is, frankly, where God outdid himself. Again and again our family enjoyed first views of Rainier that night. Just over a ridge, through the towering fir, or around another bend we witnessed the vast south face of its Emmons and Ingraham glaciers.

Silent and sullen, massive and majestic, the mountain always has its mysterious charm, its captivating appeal, its constant presence. Rainier mesmerizes those who love beauty, changes colors for the bored, and laughs at those who desire its summit.

I should know. I lived where Rainier beckoned me long enough to inspire me and inspired me long enough to teach me. You cannot look at Rainier without appreciating God, nor climb it without respecting disappointment. Mountain climbing offers a strange lesson for those who attempt to reach summits: hope is always strengthened when it meets with hardship.

By now my hope should be quite strong; I tried to summit Rainier four times and failed. What a wondrous mix of inspiration and lesson: If you can learn from disappointment, it will temper the mettle of your hope. The learning is not cheap, for disappointment is not fun. But it can be fruitful.

A disappointment can merely let you down, throw you for a loop, or send you into a tailspin. It can be as minor as a case of the blues or as major as a loss of hope.

The death of an old saint brings a certain measure of understandable joy. But tragic losses—a child's death, one's self-esteem or virginity, a divorce, a reputation—may so cloud our perspective that confidence can be lost in God. If we deal honestly with our disappointments, they can teach us lessons we will never learn on the sunny summits of victory.

Paul would understand if anybody would. Read Rom. 5:1-5 and you will see how he deals with disappointment and hope. Hear the key part: "We also rejoice in our sufferings, because we know that suffering produces perseverance; perseverance, character; and character, hope. And hope does not disappoint us, because God has poured out his love into our hearts by the Holy Spirit, whom he has given us" (vv. 3-5).

Suddenly a missed summit or two becomes quite insignificant compared to life's major disappointments. But disappointments, whether they stem from setback, sorrow, regret, anger, failure, or hurt can serve to undo our confidence if our hope is not firmly fixed in the Lord. Look at the basis of our hope:

First, rejoice (be thankful) in the midst of the trial (or failure). Praising God may be a cinch when things are going well, but otherwise it is a choice. Paul said to just do it. Rejoicing has its focus upon God: "And we rejoice in the hope of the glory of God" (Rom. 5:2). But its timing is in the middle of misery ("in our sufferings," v. 3). What a lesson!

Second, misery has a meaning. Suffering produces perseverance, which produces character, which produces hope. What a victorious cycle! Only with the Spirit's help are we able to see the tragedy of some terrible disappointment end in hope.

Third, mountains are capricious, having no sense of justice. But God brings justice, however delayed. God will usually allow "mountains" to exert their authority (weather, avalanches) in this life, so He understands our disappointment and misery. But one day our disappointment shall have a little meeting with His justice. The scales will be balanced. God will rule.

A day is coming when God will mingle mercy with grace and convert failure and disappointment into victory. So even if all we see are the losses, the mistakes, the hurts, the missed summits, we should remember something: Through the fog of our huge heartache and small regret, just beneath the glory of some hidden summit, God waits. Justice is on His mind. He's gonna win.

11 Endurance

The Fabled False Summit of Mount Adams

Every now and then we glimpsed the majestic south face of the mountain. Over the rocky path and around the massive boulders we hiked, inching ever so slowly toward the broad base of Adams. Left, right. Left, right. While each step brought us closer to the summit, the climb was always uphill and exhausting. It was my first mountain climb, and I couldn't understand the slow, tortoiselike pace of Dr. George and Larry Harper and Ed Johnson. I was eager to get up high. They seemed so deliberate.

After six hours I understood: Climbing was arduous work, and extreme physical demands would be made. Before dawn the next morning we were on the enormous snowfield, roped together for a 3,000-foot ascent to the 12,237-foot summit. On and on we climbed—thinner air, altitude sickness (headache and nausea), loss of appetite. The sun was hot and reflected off the white snowfield.

Suddenly I saw the sharp line of the great summit of Mount Adams, a masterpiece of God. Every step was a breath, every move an effort, less than 20 yards now! Finally . . . the summit. Then I turned around and could not believe my eyes. Across a huge valley, perhaps half a mile away, was the true summit of Mount Adams with another 600 feet straight up to finish. I was only on the "false summit." Sheer perseverance enabled us to finish.

I lived 45 years before that July summit day and have lived 5 years since. Nothing, for me, parallels the need for endurance in the Christian life like mountain climbing. God's wonder, Christian fellowship, self-reliance, dependence—it's all there. But the strain of effort, the will to persevere or "the pull of doing what is tough," as Ann Kiemel says, defines climbing . . . and the Christian's walk. Listen to Ann:

> Not everyone needs to run ten miles a day . . . or abstain totally from sweets, or meditate with God an hour and one-half early in the morning. But, everyone should feel the stretch, the pull of doing what is tough. Not that which is easy, but that which will refine and enhance life. Life is not made up of big moments, but ordinary days where there is no one to pat you on the back, or cheer you on, or notice you. You must give your best on ordinary days, and the big moments will come only now and then.[4]

Endurance. Perseverance. Whether in mountain climbing, personal devotions and prayer, or just holding on until you reach the summit, give your best on the ordinary days. None may see, applaud you, or show that they care. But God sees your climb, the tough work you're doing. Some days His grace and your endurance will be all that gets you through.

There are easy ways out. Friends care, and when you are just not feeling well, accept their generosity. But do not let yourself be too easy on yourself. Take the risk of going on up the hill by holding the best attitude you can in your situation, by returning bigness of soul for pettiness of surrounding.

In *The Last Step: The American Ascent of K2,* Rick Ridgeway quotes René Daumal: "Keep your eye fixed on the path to the top, but don't forget to look in front of you. The last step depends on the first. Don't think you're there just because you see the summit. Watch your footing, be sure of the step, but don't let that distract you from the highest goal. The first step depends on the last."[5] I am truly humbled by that.

"The last step depends on the first." Or, to reach any summit, you have to take that first step. Common sense. "The first steps depends on the last." Absolutely! Unless the last and final steps (toward heaven, emotional healing) motivate us, we will never take the first step toward our goal.

Those who love you want to know if you will be faithful in your steps. Will you be challenged enough by the last step to take the first step? Will you "run with perseverance the race marked out"? (Heb. 12:1). Don't be fooled by false summits. Once you've arrived, you may have a little farther to go.

12 Fear

One Misty Night at Bear Camp

We lay perfectly still. "Shh. Did you hear that?" I asked my son. "Well, I think so, but I'm not sure. Did you hear anything?" Steve responded. Except for raindrops against the wall of our two-man tent, it was quiet. The night was pitch black, the sky moonless, the wind soft. Our food, placed in bear-bags, hung high overhead in a tree just up the trail from our tent.

Suddenly we heard it again, that unmistakable growl of a bear. "Hey, listen, this time I heard it and it was closer!" Steve said. "Remember the rule," he reminded, "just bang a couple of eating plates together, and they'll usually run off."

"Well, I have another rule," I rejoined. "We ought to pray, then get out of here." But we couldn't. We were with our Boy Scout troop on a once-in-a-lifetime 10-day hike through the famous Philmont Boy Scout Ranch of northern New Mexico.

We lay quietly in the night. Off and on again the creature growled and groaned. It could be heard as it crossed first one ridge and then another, wandering about in the thick of night. After all, bears did live in this wilderness area, and our campsite was called "Bear Camp." So, brave scout adult sponsor/father/pastor that I was, I fell asleep holding a tin plate and a cup—probably the first time since childhood that I went to sleep with something in my hand.

But before we slept, neither of us had any trouble

praying. And for one simple reason—fear. How sadly strange that fear is often a greater motivator than trust. When you are in some "bear camp," an uncertain or scary place, you can turn to God.

First, we admitted our fear to one another, then to God. It does help to have someone who'll understand. But if not, confess your fear and aloneness to God. Remember, God faces everything you face because of His investment in you and His love for you. "Cast all your anxiety on him because he cares for you" (1 Pet. 5:7). Is there any anxiety or fear too big for God?

Second, our prayer was brief and specific. We prayed for protection, even divine intervention. There was a little more fervency than usual but not enough to wake up the other campers. We prayed for God to put a wall of protection around us and to guide the bear on through camp should he wander by.

Third, the next day we thanked God for His care. How important to give credit where it is due.

In reality, black bears are usually not much of a problem if campers take necessary precautions. But life requires that we sometimes camp at places of risk that threaten our security. You may be in some new environment that scares you. Perhaps the familiar surroundings of life have changed due to the death of a loved one, the loss of health or income, or a move.

Who wouldn't be afraid at such a time. What can you do?

In desperation, turn to God. But why wait until you are desperate or in some lonely outpost or in the grip of overpowering fear to turn to God? Why let fear dictate when you meet God? How much more wonderful to have a working relationship of trust with the Lord so that you and He are partners together.

The daily walks and camps of life, largely void of great danger, provide ample opportunity for the nourishment of soul through a trust relationship with God. In those quiet moments of prayer and meditation you may build a fellowship with Jesus so that when harm or change brings its test of soul you shall be ready. Don't wait until you wander into some tough and scary place to turn to God out of fear. Begin now to cultivate your trust and confidence in Him.

Take reasonable precautions and enjoy your trip through the woods of life. Fear must not keep us in or under the bed. Fear as a form of self-preservation needs to be present, but fear that overshadows our trust in God needs to be absent. Yes, there are bears. But there is God!

13 Hindrances

The Duck That Always Flew to the Left

Several years ago our local paper carried the story of a very unusual duck. Someone reported a duck with an arrow in its chest that continued to fly around one of the ponds in a city park. At last, pictures appeared in the paper. For several days we followed the saga with interest.

Finally someone named it Donna. Sure enough, Donna the Duck made the front page, soaring above the pond, wings spread, with an arrow completely through her breast! In the following days, Donna was seen resting on a rock or floating in the water. She seemed oblivious to the animal rights activists, the environmentalists, photojournalists, and others concerned about her welfare.

In fact, she continued to be the duck she always was. She nibbled at bread people threw her, she paddled about in the water. She seemed completely nonchalant about that arrow sticking through her chest. Things were fine except that when Donna took flight, she always banked to the left! No matter how far, no matter how high she went, she invariably turned to the left so much that she always came back to the same pond.

In time, the park department people brought in a specialist who got close enough to drug her and capture her. A veterinarian removed the arrow in surgery. Fortunately, the arrow missed major arteries and her heart and lungs. Donna was soon well again and from then on flew straight.

The arrow was a hindrance, an impediment to Donna's flight. She could navigate just a little, but she did not have the mobility, range of motion, and freedom necessary to be a normal duck. Thus handicapped, someone was able to capture her.

How striking is the parallel for a Christian! You don't have to have an arrow sticking through your chest to be hindered in the Lord's will or work. Any small hindrance may be used by our enemy, Satan, to defeat us.

Heb. 12:1 admonishes us: "Let us throw off everything that hinders and the sin that so easily entangles." The writer has two things in mind. First, anything, however innocent, may be an unnecessary encumbrance or weight in our walk with the Lord and our witness to others. Second, we are to renounce any specific sin that clings to us or "dogs our feet" (Phillips).

How interesting that a duck could still function—even fly—with an arrow through her chest. It is too easy to adjust to things that are not "right" for us but that may deter our walk and witness. For a while we are able to carry the extra weight by denial or even by sheer force of personality. But sooner or later the weight of little things adds up, and our capacity for spiritual endurance and direction diminishes.

We'd think by the time we were old enough to slow down in life that we'd be beyond such trials. But do not underestimate the skill of Satan. He knows we all have traits of personality, quirks of temperament, and tendencies of attitude that he can play on for our sad ruin and his sick delight.

We have to remember that Satan does not begin by shooting arrows our way. People who try to walk with the Lord, especially you who have walked with Him for some time, are frightened by his "big guns." Gross evil wakes us up.

But little inconsistencies, irritants, and short-cuts are conveniently available to the weary follower. And before we know it, we are lulled into enough lethargy that we feel at home with the arrows.

Hindrances. Oh, how small they seem. But if prayer and devotion, witness to others, and fellowship with Christ are in peril, then the entire flight of the soul will be in jeopardy. The solution is honest admission that the arrows (hindrances) need to be removed with the help of the Holy Spirit.

How reassuring to know that if we "fix our eyes on Jesus, the author and perfecter of our faith . . . [we] will not grow weary and lose heart" (Heb. 12:2-3).

14 Hurts
A Memorial to Unwanted Misfortune

I stood on the street corner, once, selling my tears.
Tears for sale! Tears for sale! I shouted till I was hoarse.
I never thought it would come to that—
the indiscriminate offering of my anguish to strangers.
But nobody wanted to buy.
The busy with hurried step, the poor with shuffling gait;
those who looked the other way and those who seemed to
          stare.
The blind next to me, yellow pencils in his black hat,
sold plenty without a word. So I shouted all the louder:
Tears for sale! Tears for sale! Get them while they're hot!
Hot with bitter failure, hot with deep regret!
Fresh from recent sorrows, folks, get them while you can!
Make you a real good deal! I hawked as best I could.
Only problem was, nobody wanted to buy.

Then He spoke softly, the blind. Why you sellin' tears,
    child?
Nobody wants more tears. Folks got enough of their own.
He stared straight ahead as he spoke,
as if to turn a head was poor economy of motion.
You just don't know, do you? I vented.
Hey, I paid a great price to get these tears. They're not
    cheap.
Got them in labeled bottles too: Tears of Remorse, Tears of
    Pain, Tears of Suspicion, Tears of Anguish, Tears of
    Hurt,
Tears of Regret, Tears of Worry, Tears of Greed, Tears of
    Anger.
Even got a double-size bottle here: Tears of Resentment.
Hey, believe me, if anybody has a right to these tears, I do.
I believe you, he said softly.
You think this is a lot, I said. Come on out to the house
    and
take a look in my basement. Got bucketfuls down there.

Works like this, I told the blind:
Somebody gives you a hurt and you don't know where to
    put it.
Somebody calls you a name and you don't know how to
    answer.
Somebody sells you a sorrow and you don't know what to
    pay.
Stranger still, some hard wind blows in out of nowhere
    filled
with unspeakable misery and you're just there:
wrong place, wrong time.
Givers of hurt, callers of names, sellers of sorrow.
Hard winds thrown in for good measure.
Before long you break the bank to pay for it all.
You begin to wonder what you've done right or wrong
or even why it came your way in the first place.
Took me a long time to collect all these bottles, see?

I rattled them in my box so he could hear with his ears the tears

he couldn't see with his eyes. He nodded silent consent.

Pour them out, he said softly. What? What did you say?

Pour them out, I said, he repeated. What? Pour them out?

Pour out my tears? You must be insane! What will I have to sell?

What will I have to talk about?

What will I have without my tears?

The blind spoke softly again: Your tears are all bitter.

You have no tears of joy, of thanksgiving, of praise, of peace.

You have no tears of forgiving, no tears of release.

You have nothing people wish to buy. Take pencils, for example.

I looked at him, this blind next to me.

Ragged, yet oddly rich. Homeless, yet strangely welcomed.

Blind, too, yet seeing afar.

He with his gathered peace; me with my scattered spirit.

He with his unsighted eyes; me with my blinded vision.

He with his empty hat; me with my stagnant bottles.

He must have heard me unscrewing the caps. Good, he said.

Watch the tears flow all the way to the gutter, he said. I did.

Let them be a memorial, he said. A memorial to what? I asked.

Let's call it the "Memorial to Unwanted Misfortune."

Not a bad name for things you don't want, right? Right, I said.

Best place to memorialize your hurts is in the gutter, he said.

Tell you what, he finished. Would you like to sell your bottles?

(See Phil. 3:13-14; Col. 3:13.)

15 Loneliness

When Nobody Ever Drops By

I look out my window a lot these days, Lord.
But I cannot look at my door.
Out the window I still see nature in the bloom of life:
the nervous sparrow, the patient robin, the towering silver
    fir.
Out the window and down a memory or two I see
the winding footpath wandering up the solemn face of
    Hood.
But I dare not look at my door.
My window is full. Full of life, full of reminder, full of
    promise.
But my door is empty. Nobody stands at my door.
Would You stand there, Lord?

Where'd You say they were, Lord?
Oh, yes, I remember now—how could I forget?
Lives of their own, people to meet, places to go, things to
    do.
So was I, once. Once. But not now.
I've lived my time; my fragile day seems nearly past.
But, I do confess, Lord, if I may,
I would like to look up at my door and see her standing
    there,
that daughter of mine, looking ever so much as her mother
    once did!
Fear to look at my door for fear she isn't there to cut my
    hair.

Seems like nobody ever drops by anymore, Lord.

It's his day to come, isn't it, God, that son of mine?
Can't wait to see him, strong in the vigor of his middle-
    aged years. Looks mighty young to me. It's his day, I
    think, Lord!
Almost hesitate to watch, God,
for fear there'll be no shadow to darken the door.
Seems like nobody ever drops by anymore, Lord!
But out the window and down a decade or two
I see the gray bobber dancing high up Eagle Creek Pass
    way.
Got my old memories, Lord,
but I'd rather have somebody at my door.
Seems like nobody ever drops by anymore, Lord.

Well, You know me, God. Dare say I've complained more
than I should! No harm meant; just lonely, Lord, just lone-
    ly.
Got plenty enough to thank You for, Father—
warm place here, food to eat, old potted plant that never
    dies.
Eyes to see, Lord, too. My thanks for them!
Look at her last picture in my Bible every day.
But out the window and down an age or so
I see the youthful bride, the children in their play.
God, I wish they'd cross the door just once again! Just
    seems
like almost nobody ever drops in.

Nobody never, nobody ever drops by? Why that can't be.
Looks like some child scribbled a flower on my papers.
So he came with his mother after all. Now I remember.
And what's this note left here on my little bed?
Must have slept straight through, while they visited me in-
    stead.
Can't say nobody ever drops by now, can I?
Perhaps I want more company than I need,

or even have some I don't remember. Old minds fool old
   men.
And yet, set up here as I am this way,
it just seems like almost nobody ever drops by.

Who knows? The call, the wait, the door ajar
might bring some old friend from off afar.
But old friends now are long since gone, and here I am left
   alone.
Can't look at the door all that much, You understand.
But when I do, Lord, You're waiting there with joy astir
As if to say you always were.
But out the window and down a time or two,
I'll take the trail I used to take,
I'll hold the memories I used to make,
and see if I can stay awake
in case someone drops by.
(See Josh. 1:5, 9.)

16 Loss

Mistaking God's Silence for His Absence

While in my first pastorate I left home in near whiteout
conditions to hold a youth revival. When I returned, I discovered that a young man in our congregation had been
injured at work. At the hospital I learned that his accident
resulted in the detachment of both retinas. Each of us en-
dured moments of blindness on the same day. Mine ended
nearly as soon as it began. His blindness has continued,
now, for nearly 25 years.

   Thus entered into my life not only a man, Walt Augustat, but a mysterious and perplexing aspect of God's nature—His silence in the presence of our many requests for
His intervention. And with passing time, another discovery:

the ability of the human spirit to distinguish between God's silence and His absence.

Now, Walt and his wife, Shirley, are not the kind of people who would want to be lionized, placed on a pedestal, or fussed over. But it is a lesson, a powerful one, for all of us to see that ordinary people, with God's grace, are capable of handling extraordinary burdens without forsaking Him. In Walt's case, 25 years seems fair enough proof of that. While God is to be exalted in this or any other account of human triumph, God could not be exalted were there no "candidate" available and capable.

The fact that there are no volunteers for God's grace to be so modeled only underscores our understandable humanity. But the fact that a Walt Augustat has risen out of relative obscurity to display such grace underscores God's vast, if silent, interest.

I wasn't there for you when you lost your child, when you were raped, when your spouse died, or when your son never came back from the war. But I was there to see our brother Walt mature through misery to stability. Guess who else was there?

Perhaps the most perplexing thing about God is also the most reassuring—His presence. We cannot see Him, we cannot touch Him, sometimes we cannot hear Him. But regardless of our mortal "cannots," God still is. Some would say that we cannot prove God's presence; how, then, could we prove His absence in our lives? God's silence would no more imply His absence than the silence of a friend who didn't answer when you spoke.

My wife, Karen, is quite patient with me as I rattle on, and sometimes she answers me. Sometimes, but not always. She does not need to speak for me to know she is there.

We learn by faith that God does not need to display His power in order to maintain it, lay claim to it, or be God. God's ability sometimes stands apart from His demonstration, seeing what I see in the real world of crowded hospitals, nursing care facilities, and prisons. If God has the ability and we have the faith, then why aren't more of the sick made whole and the wicked cleansed? Why does God answer some prayers and remain silent in response to others? Am I to believe that I have too little faith or that God is mad at me or that He isn't there at all?

In a day when God seems to be so easily approached and when His power is so quickly demonstrated in healings, it can be perplexing. Asking why is normal, but I must not get stuck in the "Why?" trap. My role is not to second-guess God. My joyful duty is to present my case, rest in the assurance that Jesus is my Intercessor, and know that God does not need to answer my prayer to still be God. I must rejoice in the apparent victories of others who are helped, and remain faithful in the meantime.

Never forget: God keeps the ledger books. He is responsible for loss as well as gain. He never comes up short. We rejoice with those who rejoice. But those who weep, including you, deserve a certain measure of respect for holding true in the midst of great and awesome loss. God is not so capricious as to select certain people to suffer loss. But those who endure trials faithfully experience grace in a way others do not.

There are two kinds of people who scare me. Those who have God all figured out, and those who don't believe in Him at all. If you've sometimes not understood or thought God had a hearing problem, at least you know there is a God. (See Isa. 43:1-3.)

17 Memories

Day of the Crying Pines

The wind blew softly, carrying the aroma of freshly tilled spring soil across the fertile fields. The air was muggy, as usual in the South. The atmosphere inside the crowded country chapel was oppressive, the morning sun hot.

People had gathered for the funeral of a child. Difficult enough as it was, circumstances were all the more unbearable for the father because he blamed himself for the loss of his son. My father served as the minister for this sad occasion. In the mysterious providence of God, I, too, attended that funeral.

It was not an easy day. After dismissal, I stood outside in the yard alone. I distinctly remember the seeming contrast between the sorrow inside that little church and the joy outside. Inside were bitter tears of loss and regret. Outside were all the sights and sounds and smells of springtime in bloom.

Yet, I remember thinking that if this earthly father cried, perhaps our Heavenly Father cried too. In my boyish mind, even the dogwoods and long-needle pines seemed to nod their agreement in grief as the breeze blew.

That was nearly 40 years ago. I am not sure I have learned much in life, but I am certain that God is touched with our grief and sorrow. And I like to think He reminded me so that morning in my youth that I recall as the day of the crying pines.

Memories. Sometimes joyous, sometimes sacred, sometimes tragic. There are memories we'd like to remember. There are memories we wish we could forget. If God permits us to live long enough, we collect memories that need to be healed.

First, healing comes through remembering. This is painful. The hurts, the injustices—both the ones given to us and the ones we have given to others—need to be consciously recalled. Perhaps we were taught to "stuff our feelings," to bury them deep within our spirit. Suppression of the junk of life means we have to carry it around. We can't see it, but others may find in us attitudes of anger or resentment. If, to protect and defend our theology or public witness, we are forced into denial, then healing is stalled. It is better to remember hurt with honest humility than to deny it with false pride.

Second, healing comes through confessing memories. How liberating to tell our loving Heavenly Father anything. Have you ever known anybody who confessed something to God and lost his place at God's table? Confession introduces us to accountability when we confide in a trustworthy friend, counselor, or pastor. Just as God's physical healing often includes a physician, so our emotional healing may include counselors. A good counselor respects God and helps you verbalize emotions and feelings. Our "Wonderful Counselor" (Isa. 9:6) listens and cares.

Third, healing comes through releasing memories, but only after confessing them. Perhaps, in a technical sense, the mind has everything stored in its computer, and we never truly forget. But the Holy Spirit is stronger than the human mind, and He can enable us to refuse to dwell upon painful memories. We need not go over them or play them back like an old worn-out cassette. There is a difference between forgetting and releasing.

Then, once this is done, we ask God to help us let go of the memory. We have to make a conscious choice not to camp out by our forgiven sins, mistakes, hurts, and errors of judgment. Like the invalid man of Bethesda, Jesus may also ask you, "Do you want to get well?" (John 5:6). One of the most destructive things we do to ourselves and others is to constantly recall and verbalize all the old wounds we inflicted upon ourselves or others or received from others. Let go and be cleansed!

Through restitution, apology, confession, or even loving confrontation you may be able to go back and make right something that came out wrong. We are never too young to be hurt. We are never too old to be healed. Tears of sorrow for hoarded hurt. Tears of joy for released wrongs. If pines "weep," what of God?

18 Patience

The Virtue That Carries a Lot of Wait

A few years ago we had a dog named Skippy and a cat named Ernie. Skippy was a Chihuahua and Ernie was whatever cats usually are. Skippy was nervous, high-strung, and was out of breath after barking four times. He had eyes like headlights on a '47 Buick. Ernie was lazy, insolent, and a living definition of indifference. They got along amazingly well, mainly because Ernie was so patient with the dog. Skippy would run circles around the cat, make all kinds of racket, and never do any harm. The old cat would just lie there, largely disinterested. Ernie's patience made up for Skippy's impatience.

I am trying to be more like Ernie—not indifferent, but patient. Perhaps it is a personality trait, but I am one of those souls who needs more patience. Not only do I need it with others, but I need it toward myself and God as well.

Lamentations is not my favorite book of the Bible, but it was written for people like me—people who are too impatient for God to do His (often) slow work, for life to bring its slow justice, for time to heal the deep wounds. God is patient with me, more than I deserve. It can be truly said that patience is a virtue that carries a lot of weight, but especially "wait."

I have often thought that God's greatest attribute is patience: the "Waiting Father," He has had to be for all us prodigals to come to Him. He even waits for us to mature. Just as soon as we come to Him, there He is, waiting to be

God for us. Not that we should (or ever may) take His grace for granted. It is just that while we are impatiently chasing our rainbows, licking our wounds, or whatever, God yearns for the day of our return.

When you read Lam. 3:19-40, you see how God weaves His patient will into our scattered ways. *First, I am thankful that God is merciful if I wander.* Verse 19 says, "I remember my affliction and my wandering, the bitterness and the gall." I don't believe Christians can wander off from God and still remain Christians forever. But I think the Lord's people sometimes get too impatient with God to heal their sorrow, and they wander around in their discouragement. I have. But listen to the writer's solutions: "I well remember [my wandering and bitterness], and my soul is downcast within me. Yet . . . I have hope" (vv. 20-21). Can we be more patient to receive His mercy when we wander?

Next, I am glad that the Lord is faithful if I wait. Here's one of the Bible's great promises for all of us impatient people: "His compassions never fail. They are new every morning; great is your faithfulness. I say to myself, 'The Lord is my portion; therefore I will wait for him'" (3:22-24). "Wait for Him!"

Our society (and sometimes even the church) values success, productivity, and maybe even a dash of the spectacular. Nobody means any harm. Perhaps it is a kind of corporate impatience, one of the ways we try to show our zeal for the Lord. But do you know what pleases the Lord most of all? It is patient waiting on our part for Him to be faithful to us. Sometimes I try so hard to help God get on with His program. I should do my part. But I should let Him be God.

Last, I am glad God is just there when I suffer. All of us suffer more than we are willing to admit. But we can suffer before the Lord because He won't laugh at us or forsake us. God would understand because He has allowed our suffering. "Though he brings grief, he will show compassion, so great is his unfailing love. For he does not willingly bring affliction or grief to the children of men" (3:32-33). How wonderful that God's compassion makes Him agonize over what His will permits! Even now you can trust God where you are to "be there for you" in your suffering, making the best offer He can: himself. His unfailing love.

Discover His mercy in your impatience. Express your despair and appreciate His awesome faithfulness. Then let God be God. "But they that wait upon the Lord shall renew their strength" (Isa. 40:31, KJV). Patience carries a lot of "wait." But it's worth the weight.

19 Pilgrimage

The Danger of Arriving Before You Get There

What is it about trains? In my early childhood we used to travel between Texarkana, Kansas City, and Topeka to visit our grandparents. Memories are filled with the long and lonely night whistle and the rhythmic clacking of wheel to steel as we journeyed through villages and farmlands, sleepy with honest toil. By day we asked the conductor to show us his gold Hamilton pocket watch, and we rode backward in the dining car during supper.

As children we enjoyed walking the aisles, studying odd facial features of passengers. Never a dull moment for us. We rode the platform between cars, and watched the stars at night from the dome car. The next morning at Wichita, we pressed our faces against the window to watch the iceman pull his dripping delivery cart up to the diner.

Destination? Topeka and Grandma's, but that was two days and half a childhood away to us. We had better things to do. Like ride the famous Kansas City Southern.

Where and when did I lose it, this capacity to feel the moment, to appreciate the tangible? When did I forget that the stuff of life was a plowed field and a small reunion on the wooden steps of the station at Junction City?

Somewhere between then and now—between youth and age, between college and graduate schools, parenting, pastoring, and publishing—that's where. Somewhere along the way the destination became the goal, whereas in my childhood the joy was in the journey. Somehow the result, the consequence, the bottom line became the focus rather than the process of getting there. My algebra teacher said before tests, "Show me on paper how you get your answer." Somewhere the what had exceeded the how.

The danger of being "goal only" oriented is that you may arrive before you get there. Sounds impossible on the surface. Who in their right mind could have a body in one place and their heart in another? How could you be bodily on the train but already at the station emotionally? Or in the middle of a trek up the backside of a mountain with your mind on the summit? I am afraid I'd qualify for all of the above.

This isn't a plea to live only for the moment; the Lord knows enough people live meaningless lives, void of focus and direction. But it is an appeal to shun the tragedy of missing the moment altogether—of missing the opportunities and even the stern disciplines of heartache because we are hard in the chase of accomplishment.

So we strive for balance. We keep our affection fixed on the goal, but we keep our attention fixed in the here and now. We do need commitment for heaven, for example, but we must be of some earthly good at the same time. While there is ultimate achievement, there is also immediate awareness. The biblical Hebrew heroes modeled this very well. Abraham "was looking forward to the city with foundations, whose architect and builder is God" (Heb. 11:10). At the same time, "When called to go . . . [he] obeyed and went, even though he did not know where he was going" (v. 8). Moses was life-focused because "he chose to be mistreated along with the people of

God rather than to enjoy the pleasures of sin for a short time" (v. 25). Yet he also "was looking ahead to his reward" (v. 26).

Heaven awaits the forgiven faithful—just around a bend or two. When we're there, we'll have arrived. But until then, we have to remember that we don't arrive when we join a church, become a Christian, experience sanctification, discover gifts, or do great things for God. The journey begins at those points.

We do well when we practice faithfulness in the long, dark night, when we exercise respect toward "conductors" in authority over us, when we learn to laugh at our own quirks and hurts and make it easy for others to laugh too.

We do well when we overlook our own date with public fame or private fear and become available for the unexpected joys and miseries of our pilgrimage. Who knows? The man with the ice cart might have a broken heart. So don't arrive before you get there.

20 Providence

Did You Ever Wonder Why?

Did you ever wonder why? I have. When my friend Bill Fields died, Dad said to me: "Life is full of unanswerable whys. It is better to ask, 'What can I do in response?'"

In one pastorate our church buried a teenager annually. The death of William Burgess in Champaign at age 94 was understandable, but not the death of Bob Chenoweth (and his four associates) in Flint at age 49. We struggle when tragedies are untimely (an early death), accidental (unplanned), unnecessary (rape or murder), random (Tylenol tampering), or excessive (the Holocaust). We wonder about such tragedies because we are human and because we care.

We know God rejoices and suffers along with us. If

His Spirit can be grieved (Eph. 4:30), we know God has feelings. Certainly in Jesus, God understands completely our humanity. God also comforts us as we suffer. "Praise be to . . . the God of all comfort, who comforts us in all our troubles, so that we can comfort those in any trouble with the comfort we ourselves have received from God" (2 Cor. 1:3-4). We, then, share our comfort.

At the heart of God's nature rests His providential interest and care regarding those He loves most—us! We must know the difference between God's perfect and His permissive will for our lives. God's perfect will always includes our salvation, our spiritual maturity, and whatever else He may choose to reveal to us. His perfect will is quite specific. But His permissive will is broad; that is, God permits (and tolerates) many things none of us like. His permissive will is often hard to bear.

When God's permissive will brings sunshine, I can handle it. But when His will brings thunderstorms (heartache), I get uncomfortable. I want God to intervene when it seems necessary to me. But if He doesn't, do I still trust Him as my loving Heavenly Father? God performs miracles, but not always—and not even usually. Rarely does God seem to tilt the playing field of life in our favor. On the other hand, only God knows the many times He has intervened when we never knew it. Doesn't God ever wonder about the things He permits?

Because God is God, He knows exactly what He is up to. He is a God of order, not of disarray. His decisions and movements are purposeful. Our lack of understanding reveals our frailty. He alone is divine. If God is loving, He gets no satisfaction out of our misery; therefore, He hurts when we hurt. He is more than willing to suffer with us, just as He once suffered for us. The understandable confusion and wonder is on our side of eternity. On God's side is a vast master plan we have never seen.

Since we don't understand God's ways, sometimes all we seem to do is wonder. If God permits a miracle, we wonder in awe and marvel at Him. But if He permits a tragedy, we sometimes wonder in uncertainty and doubt. Why? Because our human frailty cannot make sense of His divine order. If God loved us while we were in sin (Rom. 5:8), why wouldn't He love us when we are in doubt or uncertainty? Wondering why is understandable. But it could become disrespectful and lead to distrust if we did not finally bring our unanswered whys, and our right to them, to the Lord.

When God makes no sense at all, we do what seems humanly strange—we trust the God we cannot understand. The depth of our relationship with God is measured not so much by what we understand of His will but by how much we trust His judgment.

Let the Bible speak again: "And we know that in all things God works for the good of those who love him, who have been called according to his purpose" (Rom. 8:28). God's perfect will is ideal. His circumstantial (permissive) will is real—sometimes a real nightmare for us, but also a real opportunity for Him to do what He does best: stand by in tough times. His ultimate will is realized when we make heaven our home.

There will be times we do not even like God's decisions, let alone comprehend them. But if we can yield what we do not see, like, and understand to His care and keeping, at least it will be up to God to be there for us. When His judgment is finally trusted and our frailty is finally confessed, God will finally be God.

21 Resiliency

And After the Stone-wind . . . Almost Nothing

I have never been to the moon, but I have been close. When we lived in Washington State our family visited the famous "blowdown" area caused by the eruption of Mount Saint Helens. Once considered one of the most beautiful mountains in the Cascade Range, Saint Helens is 1,200 feet shorter than its original 9,677 feet, due to its volcanic explosion on May 18, 1980.

When we rounded the corner we could not believe our eyes. Two hundred thirty square miles of devastation, including 150 square miles of stripped and leveled trees, and everything covered with a thick layer of gray ash that made it resemble a moonscape. We had visited my wife's parents in 1980 in Spokane, Wash., 350 miles away, where ash was plowed off major roads.

When an earthquake triggered an avalanche on Saint Helens, the mountain was ripped open, exposing super-heated steam and magma. The blast forced rock out of the opening, with winds over 200 miles an hour. One hundred eighty foot firs would not normally fall or be completely stripped like toothpicks even in high winds. But the wind carried rocks and boulders as large as cars. The result was what geologists called a "stone-wind,"[6] a wind of steam and rock, which blew sideways out of Saint Helens for 15 minutes.

As far as the eye could see, desolation. What could survive a stone-wind? Nothing! Well, almost. Just days later were clear evidence of life: trillium and huckleberry, sedge and fireweed, termites and pocket gophers, purple lupine and Indian paintbrush. What accounts for it? Another of God's wonders typical of His nature—the resiliency of life. Resiliency is simply the ability to survive, to hold on, to bounce back in the face of great stress. It is recovering from the extra weight of misfortune—like winter trees under ice.

If God helps His created world survive the forces of nature, then what of His children created in His likeness? We cannot help being in the wrong place at the wrong time. We cannot control the sudden quakes and avalanches that come roaring down our path. But there is within the justice of God the assurance not only that He is caught with us in our misfortune (remember Jesus!) but also that He helps us cope and perhaps recover.

While it is normal (even necessary) to admit and deal rightly with our anger, wounded pride, and misery, our healing is advanced if we ask God to give us a resilient attitude. Paul certainly had his hard times, but listen to his encouragement: "We are hard pressed on every side, but not crushed; perplexed, but not in despair; persecuted, but not abandoned; struck down, but not destroyed" (2 Cor. 4:8-9). How wonderful!

That's sort of like saying, "Yeah, if I lose my job, I still have my health; if I lose my health, I'm still alive; if I get cancer, I get cancer; if I was raped, I did survive; if I'm dying, that's about all that can go wrong; if I'm not ready to die, there is even a solution for that!"

Don't be fooled. Resiliency is tough stuff. This is not a pie-in-the-sky form of denial. It takes a considerable amount of courage and effort to be a survivor. For some people, death is not the enemy, and may be a welcomed friend. But for the living, the issue is hanging on and bending without breaking as long as God gives us breath.

If you feel you are going to snap and all ground is about to give way beneath your feet, it does not mean you are a spiritual failure and something less than good. God does not have some high-level breaking point designed to alienate you from His love. We are mortals, and if caught in some hurt or stone-wind beyond our power to cope, we don't have to be powerful to be resilient. We bend and stretch until it's over.

Remember the little flowers trapped in the awful force of Saint Helen's stone-wind. They just stayed still. When the wind blew, they bent. When the ash fell, they sagged. When the fire raged, they survived. Resiliency is, after all, finishing well.

22 Security

Does God Weigh Enough?

Nelson Kunz and Tom Ireland have both kindly taken me on tours of Buick's Final Assembly Plant here in Flint. Our town is known as "Buick City," because the Buick LeSabre and Oldsmobile 88 Royale are both made here.

The assembly line, with its constant and methodical movement of parts and pieces, is fascinating. Conveyors and belts, chains and hoists, provide a steady flow of unassembled items. The list seems endless: frames, fenders, doors, dashboards, and engines. One designs engines, another welds seams. One paints, another assembles, and yet another inspects. And at the end of an hour, about 65 new LeSabres roll off the line.

One of our guides said, "And over here is 'The Rock.' We put cars on it to check for dimensional accuracy. The Rock gives absolute zero distortion; that is, it remains unchangeable and offers a nearly perfect platform for measurement. When they want a place that is rock-solid with absolutely no movement, they come here. Solid granite. Weighs 70 tons."

The Rock, inside the Dimensional Verification Center, was wider and longer than a full-size car, and I estimated about three or four feet thick. Granite is an especially dense quartz rock tempered by volcanic heat and formed by the solidification of molten magma. Tough stuff. Rock hard. Seventy tons. Talk about no movement. That's 140,000 pounds of still.

Does God weigh that much? How much security can He offer? In our day of shifting principles and faltering heroes, what does God offer in the way of solid security? Edward Mote affirmed, "When all around my soul gives way, He then is all my hope and stay." Does God weigh enough to balance out my insecurity?

When I was a senior in high school, Mother had a leadership role in our young peoples' meetings on Sunday nights. This was in the late '50s in Canton, Ohio. We always ended the evening quoting Ps. 19:14 (KJV in those days). "Let the words of my mouth, and the meditation of my heart, be acceptable in thy sight, O Lord, my strength, and my redeemer."

About 50 of us quoted it in unison weekly. There has been since then, for me, a reverence about who God was . . . and is. As our strength, God is more than a match for our weakness; as our redeemer, more than enough for our sin. But my public words and private thoughts are to honor Him, seeing the weight of His worth.

How wonderful, then, that the NIV translates the word "strength" in verse 14 as "Rock"! I can verify it. Looking at a 70-ton rock my first thought was, "Now there's a rock no car could budge!"

Sooner or later all of us tire of the relative and need the absolute. We grow weary with things that shift, and we seek the solid. We need someplace where the footing is safe, where the measurements are sure, where the decisions are just plain right. You may not be so fortunate as to fly to "Buick City" where you can have a look at "The Rock" anytime you desire. But there is another Rock to whom you may fly. His accuracy exceeds granite. His dwelling place is more sophisticated than the Dimensional Verification Center. His weight of eternal glory surpasses 70 tons. The Psalmist called Him "the rock of my strength" (62:7, KJV), "the rock of my salvation" (89:26, KJV), "the rock of my refuge" (94:22, KJV), and "the rock that is higher than I" (61:2, KJV).

More than 70 tons. Do you think God "weighs" more than that? "The Rock" at Buick City weighs more than 70 times the weight of a full-size car. How much more God weighs than you and the things that make you insecure. How solid His love and fair His judgment.

Next time you think about the way cars are built, remember the little slab of granite we have over here in Flint. Next time you feel insecure in your soul, remember the Rock of Ages.

No wonder we call Him God.

23 Self-esteem
A Cry of Worth from Room 431

Some years ago I walked up the sidewalk of a rather humble home to make a pastoral call. The yard had an assortment of used furniture and the undeniable trivia of poverty.

There I met a very kind, nearly apologetic lady in her mid-60s. She went to our church, but she went to the hospital a lot more often. First one thing and then another. Never in my ministry have I seen such human misery, nor so patient a spirit. Some people just have woes. She had many woes—serious physical problems, financial worries, sarcastic children, and a verbally cruel husband. I never understood how she survived.

So I asked her one day, "How do you handle it? What's the secret to your ability to bear up?" We were in her hospital room visiting. Room 431. "Well, it's Jesus. He bears up for me. He sure must love me a lot to not forsake me," she said.

Remembering her misery, I was caught off guard. Finally, I repeated, "So you don't feel like God has forsaken you?"

"Oh, no. He's my best friend. Sometimes about my

only friend. Nobody in my family thinks much of me. But my value is in what God thinks of me and not in what I'm not. When you're not worth much to others, you're still worth a lot to Him." Wow! Did I hear that? What an amazing cry of worth from one thought to be so worthless. God takes note when sparrows fall. Then Jesus says, "Are you not much more valuable than they?" (Matt. 6:26). Have we underestimated our true worth?

I prayed, thanked her, and left feeling like she had helped me. "My value is in what God thinks of me and not in what I'm not." Where did she learn that? How do you teach that concept of God to people? How do you rise up out of such utter human failure and sorrow with a view that your true worth and real value is in the God who cares and not in what you could never be?

This dear woman learned that her self-esteem was rooted in Jesus Christ. In a sense, she felt her true value was somehow out of herself. She knew the sad family pain of personal rejection. Her value was not in what others thought of her. It was in what God knew her to be in Jesus—His redeemed daughter! As far as cries of worth go, hers goes pretty far.

So many people in good health and in the best of times struggle with false perceptions of their self-worth. If they only had this or that, if they only knew so-and-so as a friend, then life would be better. Then when sickness or trouble comes, their already low self-esteem plunges even further. Why? Their self-esteem is based in what others think of them, not in what God thinks of them.

My suffering friend knew who she was in Jesus—somebody important enough not to be ignored. Her value to herself pivoted in that great concept. She knew God loved her as she was—poor, miserable, physically unattractive, and sickly.

The issue is not sickness or wellness, not happiness or unhappiness. The issue is believing that our self-esteem and value to God lies in what He thinks of us, not in what others think of us or in what we'd like to be but humanly cannot be.

One of Dad's sermons contained this poem.

> *I would rather be a "could-be"*
>   *if I could not be an "are";*
> *For a "could-be" is a "may-be"*
>   *with a chance of reaching par.*
> *I would rather be a "has-been"*
>   *than a "might-have-been" by far,*
> *For a "might-have-been" has never been,*
>   *but a "has-been" was once an "are."*[7]

I saw a lot of misery in Room 431. I thought the poor old soul was in her mid-60s until I later learned she was only 44. So be cheered, my friend. If you are not healthy, not happy, or not hopeful, just remember: Your worth is not in what you're not. It is in whose you are and what He thinks about you.

24 Self-sufficiency

Roped Together on Hood's South Face

Our summit day on Mount Hood (11,245 feet) in north-west Oregon was absolutely breathtaking. White-bright glaciers, deep blue sky, fabulous views of Adams, Saint Helens, and Rainier—all mountains in southwest Washington—were the rewards of a fruitful climb.

Dr. George Harper, my lead-partner, and I were alone on top. We left the parking lot about 2:30 A.M. that morning and wandered up the glacier on Hood's south face. We passed a bergschrund (a massive crack in the glacier) and places where the strong odor of sulphur hung thick in the air. We ascended Hogsback Ridge, a prominent spine extending upward toward the massive head of Hood until we reached a steep 50-degree icy chute.

Finally we summited, signed the register, took pictures, and prepared for descent. Climbing up was mainly strenuous. Climbing down was strenuous and, in places, dangerous.

The icy chute, in descent, demanded some technical skill on George's part due to length and pitch. George, an experienced mountaineer, was very cautious, carefully explaining each step. I began the descent, stepping backward, inching my way with crampons (steel spikes) strapped to boots. Ice axes aided balance and grip in the chute, and we were fastened by rope to one another in case of a slip. I was given just enough rope to feel my partner's presence, yet enough to move at my own rate. He remained firmly planted above me until I found a place to stop, dig in and belay (or hold) for him. Thus we helped one another down the steep chute until we got to Hogsback Ridge. The chute took 15 minutes to climb and nearly an hour to descend.

There is no room for self-sufficiency on mountains. All of the major mountains of the world have claimed lives. My partner kept me constantly focused on his presence in two ways. First, I felt the tug of the rope between us. Second, he frequently asked, "Is your hand through the wrist strap?" The wrist strap was a short but powerful attachment to the ice ax. If you fell and dropped your ax, at least it would still be fixed to your wrist if your hand was through the strap. Otherwise, having no ice ax to use for self-arrest would guarantee disaster.

What a wonderful parallel for those who would be partners with Christ! There is no room for independence in our walk with the Lord. We need to be close enough to God to feel the tug of His presence. God is there even when we cannot see Him, or when we are so preoccupied with putting one foot in front of the other that we have no conscious thought of His whereabouts. For some, the great danger lies in unhooking from God altogether and going their own way. For others, the desire may be for a longer rope in order to venture off on their own, and then depend upon God only in the emergency of some steep and icy way.

But for too many of us the danger is that, while we may remain hooked to God, we may chafe under the accountability of His tough and constant questions. The only time I felt the sudden tug of my partner's presence was when I either slipped or got too far ahead of Him. He never said a word. The rope spoke. How like God to "speak" to us.

But if George asked me once, he asked me a hundred times, "Is your hand in the wrist strap?" He knew that if I fell, at least I had a chance at self-arrest with the ax. But without the ax in hand, he alone would have to save me. And if worse came to worst on some slippery path, we could both fall.

Does God ask you hard questions about your attitude, your relationships, or your loyalty toward Him? Please don't be insulted. Consider it for your own good; He wants to prevent a fall. God wants to know: Are you prepared for dangerous descents? Are you dependent upon His Word? Are you roped to Him? "How gracious he will be when you cry for help" (Isa. 30:19).

25 Suffering

For All Your Sad Misfortune . . . I Was There

For all your hollow ventures, and all your shattered dreams,
And all your empty nothings that were bulging at the
　　　seams;
For all the broken promises and things that might have
　　　been,
For all the new beginnings you could never quite begin;
For all your sad misfortune, I was there.

For all your days of glory lying in the shattered past,
For all your darkened midnights that you feared would al-
　　　ways last;

For all the vim and vigor of your youth that slipped away,
For all the unfair misery that brought sickness and decay;
For all your sad misfortune, I was there.

For all the disappointments others dropped into your lap,
For all the roads to dialogue that took you off the map;
For all the hurts of childhood your old memory had to store,
That left you in a corner in a heap upon the floor;
For all your sad misfortune, I was there.

For all the major setbacks that you never did deserve,
For all the shining moments that you never could preserve;
For all the happy blessings and the benefits you've had,
I never missed a valley or a heartache or a sad;
For all your sad misfortune, I was there.

Yes! For all your sad misfortune, I've been there!
So bring your tattered losings that have stuck you in the
      mire,
And leave them all beside Me, here, so we can start a fire;
For all the noble visions that you had once way back then,
For all the jostled efforts—you just need to try again!
For all your unknown future, I'm still here.

For all the rousing anthems that I stirred within your
      breast,
And all the burning issues you too quickly laid to rest;
For all the crevassed glaciers that may cause your soul to
      dread,
You need only to remember that you're roped to Me in-
      stead!
For all your unknown future, I'm still here.

Give Me your fearsome phantoms, and give Me your fierce
      regret;
I'm the Artist of a painting that you've not seen even yet!
Give Me your checkered failures, the hurts that took their toll,
I wrote a book on justice, once; I don't do bad with soul.
For all your unknown future, I'm still here.

Those who doubt Me may not know Me, those who know
    Me may have fear;
But if I could move a mountain, think what I could do
    with tears!
Look high above your valley, way up high above your
    pain,
You will see the chiseled features of My glory once again!
For all your unknown future, I'm still here.

I see your sad misfortune, and I see your anguished plight,
But you must see My honor and My wisdom and My
    might!
So up from your foggy shadows! Up beyond your poor re-
    pair!
In between your sad misfortune and My summit—that is
    where,
For all your unknown future, I shall be.
(See Isa. 49:15-16.)

26 Temptation

"I'm Never Tempted to Dance, but . . ."

Grandmother lived just a few blocks from my college
dorm. One autumn Saturday I went down to visit her and
had a conversation I never forgot. She was amazingly focused for her 90 years. She spoke softly and with a pro-
nounced Southern drawl. We shifted from one topic to another. At 90 you never know how many conversations you
have left, so she wasted no time.

"Do you think people my age ever get tempted?" She
was a tried and faithful saint, had read the Bible through
perhaps 75 times, and was certainly too old and good for
such things as temptation. I was 18, full of the energies of
youth, and not prepared for discussion about sins of the

flesh. I had a narrow view of many things then, including temptation. She sensed my dilemma.

"Well, I don't know," I began. "Does the devil still tempt people your age after all the years you've walked with the Lord?"

"You understand, Jim, I'm not tempted to dance. The devil is not very smart, but he is smarter than that. Still, he does tempt me. He does not tempt me like he tempts you. Temptation is always the offer of a need we can live without."

The offer of a need we can live without. I've never heard temptation better defined. If it is a need, how can we live without it? Herein is the subtle hook of temptation. Satan knows that because we need a thing, he can make the package attractive enough to be truly tempting. That is why sins of the flesh, namely sexual impurity, are so powerfully engaging for those young enough to be interested and old enough to know better.

So Satan can devise temptation out of many things, even legitimate need. If it were not a need at all, it would not be much of a temptation. Even a wish, when fulfilled, becomes a need that gets met. So the enemy takes what he knows we want and offers it with such stunning availability that attempts at refusal are sometimes difficult even for the devout Christian.

It would have been quite easy for Grandmother, a saint, to make herself appear "spiritual" to me, a naive youth. I think Satan was testing her at this very point that morning, yet she resisted well. She could have vented her understandable anger about sexual impurity among college kids. Rather, she confessed that old-time saints still struggle with temptation.

"Impurity is not much of a problem for me at my age," she continued. "That's a problem for those who still have enough youth left in them. My problem is attitude. The devil sometimes tempts me to hold the wrong spirit, to criticize people even if they do deserve it. Dance? No, my old bones couldn't stand the strain. But attitude . . . that's where I live." Her disarming candor and depth of insight have remained with me these years.

What was the "need" Satan saw in her, however legitimate and normal, that he tried to twist for evil purposes and use as a form of temptation? Was it the need to feel important? Was it the need to exercise authority over others? Was it the need to assert spirituality? How clever of him. But how ancient a trick, for this was his very ploy against Jesus.

She shed new light on one of our favorite verses: "But each one is tempted when, by his own evil desire, he is dragged away and enticed" (James 1:14). As maturing pilgrims with the Lord, we must be willing to have a godly definition of what "need" means for us. Her statement that temptation is the "offer of a need we can live without" restricts Satan. Human need could be real without being ruler. Gratification is not the first goal.

If the fulfillment of our legitimate rights and needs is our final goal, we may be more miserable than those whose rights and needs are rarely fulfilled.

27 Trusting

"Resting Faith" for Where You Are!

When your back is against the wall, when you feel just plain rotten, or when you are going through some miserable, private hell that nobody really understands, here is a most encouraging truth—God knows how to help you rest where you are.

If He knows where you are, He knows how to reach you. If He knows how to reach you, then He surely knows how to help you.

But sometimes when you are really down, you have

neither strength nor resolve to muster that kind of trust. Faith does have an element of effort: a belief to accept, a confidence to live up to. But trust simply means, "I've done all I can do; now I rest my case." The great Andrew Murray said it well:

First, God brought me here; it is by His will I am in this straight place; in that fact I will rest.

Next, God will keep me here in His love, and give me the grace to behave as His child.

Then, God will make the trial a blessing, teaching me the lessons He intends me to learn, and working in me the grace He intends to bestow.

Last, God in His good time can bring me out again, how and when, He knows.

So: I am here 1) by God's appointment, 2) in God's keeping, 3) under God's training, and 4) for God's time.[8]

That's absolutely powerful. There is a kind of rest in faith, isn't there? When we reach the end of our strength and sometimes frantic effort, then we have to have a place to stop. Where is such a place? Exactly where you are at this moment. You may be just halfway across some dark valley, and one way out is as far as the other. Stop wherever you are right now. Realize that you are kept (sustained and guarded) by the awesome God.

The Bible's word for the discovery of your faith's resting place is *trust*. How many times have we heard it? Faith is something you have to do, have, achieve, work up, and show forth. But trusting is giving your faith a rest. In fact, trusting is the abandonment of self-involvement in faith to the point that it is all up to God. Trusting helps us rest our faith right where we are. When faith is reduced to expectation or even demand, then it gets greedy. Trust. Let faith lie with all your hopes and dreams, fears and nightmares, right where you are.

The teens in our house have abbreviated all this to the phrase "kick back"—meaning rest, trust. The other day when I expressed fatherly concern about something, one of them said, "Don't be so hyper, Dad." But, scarce with words as kids often are around parents, the other added simply, "Chill."

Kick back, chill, whatever, it all carries the same thought for things you need to let go of, just let go of. To rest your tired faith, here it is in a word: *trust* (or, chill, right?).

Ultimately, our faith, properly placed and understood, is in the person and character of God. You may be tempted to think your life and faith are on the line. Who wouldn't if you're dying or facing some great trauma? In reality, God is on the line with you, and He hasn't failed himself that I've ever heard of.

Our situation (whether good or bad) has nothing to do with God's memory, His ability, or His love. Good times do not mean He is more aware. Bad times do not mean He is less aware. God is God, meaning He is the same loving, responsible God in our misfortune as He is in our fortune. You can trust Him whether or not you feel Him, see Him, or hear from Him.

Do not be fooled: To trust God this much can be scary. The only place to trust God is, of all places, right where you are—flat on your back, in a nursing home, hitched up to wires and tubes, locked up in maximum security, stuck on a lonely outpost, or bivouacked high on a windy ridge. Trust runs both ways. Wherever you are, He is. Where He is, you need to be.

"May the God of hope fill you with all joy and peace as you trust in him" (Rom. 15:13).

28 Worry
Self-control on the Slippery Slope

Skilled mountaineers may descend a mountain by skiing, rappeling (using fixed ropes), or glissading.

The technical term *glissade* is a controlled downhill slide on snowfields where the pitch is not too steep. On our descent of Mount Adams in southwest Washington, we decided to glissade. It involved putting your feet through two holes made in the bottom of a large plastic garbage bag and pulling the bag up around your waist—much like an oversized diaper. We sat on the slope and scooted down glissade trails made by other climbers.

Having attended a self-arrest seminar, I knew that getting immediate control could be life-saving if a slip occurred. We were taught to flip over on our stomach and use an ice ax to bring quick self-arrest. The rate of descent can also be slowed by maneuvering the ice ax like a lever as you slide.

What fun it was to slide down the same snowfield in about half an hour that took nearly half a day to climb. However, I was surprised to learn that, without careful attention, you could become nearly airborne within seconds. We descended carefully, slip-sliding our way down a reasonably safe side of Mount Adams. Since the goal was not speed but control, it took considerable effort to "steer" with the ax. Gravity can always be counted on to give you a lot more speed than you need.

How true with all of life. Just about any day may bring more pain and more rain than any of us want. But, like standing on the false summit of Adams, there is nothing else to do but start down if you want to get home. That is, we have no other choice but to go on through any given day, whatever it brings us. Getting out on the slippery slope may seem risky enough, let alone sliding down it. But when things are under control . . .

Control. Insecurity or being out of control alarms us. Fear is a normal, God-given emotion for self-preservation, and whenever we are confronted with a slippery slope, some threat to our security, fear is understandable.

Fear that gets out of control becomes panic or anxiety, which is also understandable in given situations. Hence, how normal to be sure things are "in control." Even professional climbers want a safety margin that assures control. But fear that cripples our ability to cope, that prohibits our willingness to try, is worry. Worry is fretting and stewing about the unchangeable past or the unseen future.

Wisdom, forethought, and common sense will surely help. But if you are alive, you are facing risk. Not all risk can or should be avoided; otherwise, we'd never get up in the morning. Winston Churchill said, "Risk more than you can afford to lose and you will learn to play the game."[9] Risk is just there.

But we need help to control worry. We need to admit that, meticulous as we may be, we cannot control all that life will throw at us. We cannot even avoid being on life's slippery slopes, much less their degree of pitch. But we can do some things that will help us deal with the problem of worry.

First, obey the "command of commitment." "Commit your way to the Lord" (Ps. 37:5). Let God take control of your way. Not all things that sound trite are trifling. Worry is bad stuff; trust places your confidence outside yourself.

Second, laugh at the stupidity of worry. Jesus asked, "Who of you by worrying can add a single hour to his life?" (Matt. 6:27). In other words, worry will do nothing for your chances of survival if you jump out of a plane— with or without a parachute. Has worry ever been placed in worse light? Worry doesn't change things either way.

Third, don't worry about today and tomorrow at the same time. "Each day has enough trouble of its own" (Matt. 6:34). If God can care for today, He will care for tomorrow. If you fear either today or tomorrow, God will be there both days.

Notes

1. Benjamin Franklin, quoted in Gail Peterson, *The Last Laugh: A Completely New Collection of Funny Old Epitaphs* (Kansas City: Hallmark Cards, 1968), 46.

2. Harold L. Myra, "A Message from the Publisher" (Editorial), *Christianity Today* (May 17, 1985), 12.

3 No known source.

4. Ann Kiemel, *I'm Running to Win* (Wheaton, Ill.: Tyndale House Publishers, 1983), 79, 156.

5. René Daumal, quoted in Rick Ridgeway, *The Last Step: The American Ascent of K2* (Seattle: Mountaineers, 1980), front cover, inside page not numbered.

6. Patricia Lauber, *Volcano: The Eruption and Healing of Mount Saint Helens* (New York: Bradbury Press, 1986), 10.

7. No known source.

8. Attributed to Andrew Murray.

9. No known source.

Bibliography

Kiemel, Ann. *I'm Running to Win.* Wheaton, Ill.: Tyndale House Publishers, 1983.

Lauber, Patricia. *Volcano: The Eruption and Healing of Mount Saint Helens.* New York: Bradbury Press, 1986.

Peterson, Gail. *The Last Laugh: A Completely New Collection of Funny Old Epitaphs.* Kansas City: Hallmark Cards, 1968.

Ridgeway, Rick. *The Last Step: The American Ascent of K2.* Seattle: Mountaineers, 1980.

Published Article

Myra, Harold L., ed. "A Message from the Publisher." *Christianity Today,* May 17, 1985, 12.